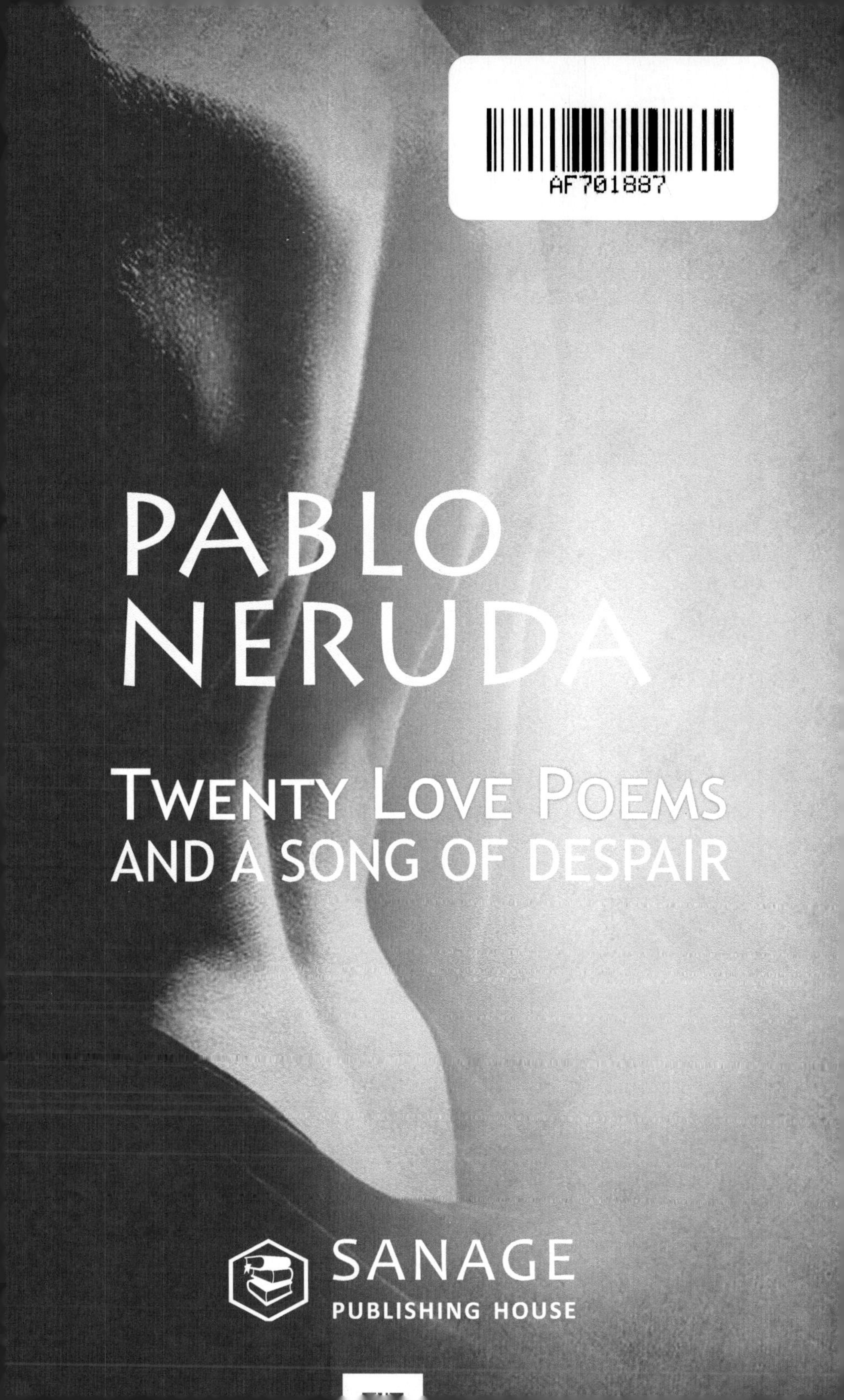

AF701887

PABLO NERUDA

TWENTY LOVE POEMS AND A SONG OF DESPAIR

SANAGE
PUBLISHING HOUSE

Copyright © 2020 Sanage Publishing House LLP

All rights reserved. No part of this publication may be reproduced, distributed, or transmitted in any form or by any means, including photocopying, recording, or other eletronic or mechanical methods, without the prior written permission of the publisher, except in the case of brief quotations embodied in critical reviews and certain other noncommercial uses permitted by copyright law. For permission requests, write to the publisher, addressed "Attention Permissions Coordinator," at the address below.

Paperback: 978-939492416-1

Any references to historical events, real people, or real places are used fictitiously. Names, characters, and places are products of the author's imagination.

Sanage Publishing House LLP
Mumbai, India

sanagepublishing@gmail.com

Pablo Neruda was the pen name and, later, legal name of the Chilean poet and politician Neftalí Ricardo Reyes Basoalto. He chose his pen name after Czech poet

Jan Neruda. Neruda became known as a poet when he was 13 years old, and wrote in a variety of styles, including surrealist poems, historical epics, overtly political manifestos, a prose autobiography, and passionate love poems such as the ones in his collection Twenty Love Poems and a Song of Despair (1924).

Pablo Neruda is often considered the national poet of Chile, and his works have been popular and influential worldwide. The Colombian novelist Gabriel García Márquez once called him "the greatest poet of the 20th century in any language.

Table of Content:

I. Body Of A Woman

Body of a woman, white hills, white thighs,
You Look like a world lying in surrender.
My rough peasant's body digs in you
and makes the son leap from the depths of the earth.

I was alone like a tunnel. The birds fled from me,
and night swamped me with its crushing invasion.
To survive myself I forged you like a weapon,
like an arrow in my bow, a stone in my sling.

But the hour of vengeance falls, and I love you.
Body of skin, of moss, of eager and firm milk.
Oh the goblets of the breast! Oh the eyes of absence!
Oh the roses of the pubis! Oh your voice, slow and sad!

Body of my woman, I will persist in your grace.
My thirst, my boundless desire, my shifting road!
Dark river-beds where the eternal thirst flows
and weariness follows, and the infinite ache.

II. The Light Wraps You

The light wraps you in its mortal flame.
Abstracted pale mourner, standing that way
against the old propellers of the twilight
that revolves around you

Speechless, my friend,
alone in the loneliness of this hour of the dead
and filled with the lives of fire,
pure heir of the ruined day.

A bough of fruit falls from the sun on your dark
garment.
The great roots of night
grow suddenly from your soul,
and things that hide in you come out again
so that a blue and pallid people,
your newly born, takes nourishment.

Oh magnificent and fecund and magnetic slave
of the circle that moves in turn through black and
gold:
rise, lead and possess a creation
so rich in life that its flowers perish
and it is full of sadness.

III. Ah Vastness of Pines

Ah vastness of pines, murmur of waves breaking,
slow play of lights, solitary bell,
twilight falling in your eyes, toy doll,
earth-shell, in whom the earth sings!

In you the rivers sing and my soul flees in them
as you desire, and you send it where you will.
Aim my road on your bow of hope
and in a frenzy I will free my flock of arrows.

On all sides I see you waist of fog,
and your silence hunts my afflicted hours;
my kisses anchor, and my moist desire nests
in you with your arms of transparent stone.

Ah your mysterious voice that love tolls and darkens
in the resonant and dying evening!
Thus in deep hours I have seen, over the fields,
the ears of wheat tolling in the mouth of the wind.

IV. The Morning Is Full

The morning is full of storm
in the heart of summer.

The clouds travel like whit handkerchiefs of goodbye,
the wind, travelling, waving them in its hands.

The numberless heart of the wind
beating above our loving silence.

Orchestral and dinive, resounding among the trees
like a language full of wars and songs.

Wind that bears off the dead leaves with a quick raid
and deflects the pulsing arrows of the birds.

Wind that topples her in a wave without spray
and substance without weight, and leaning fires.

Her mass of kisses breaks and sinks,
assailed in the door of the summer's wind.

V. So That You Will Hear Me

So that you will hear me
my words
sometimes grow thin
as the tracks of the gulls on the beaches.

Necklace, drunken bell
for your hands smooth as grapes.

And I watch my words from a long way off.
They are more yours than mine.
They climb on my old suffering like ivy.

It climbs the same way on damp walls.
You are to blame for this cruel sport.
They are fleeing from my dark lair.
You fill everything, you fill everything.

Before you they peopled the solitude that you
occupy,
and they are more used to my sadness than you
are.

Now I want them to say what I want to say to you
to make you hear as I want you to hear me.

The wind of anguish still hauls on them as usual.
Sometimes hurricanes of dreams still knock them
over.

You listen to other voices in my painful voice.

Lament of old mouths, blood of old supplications.
Love me, companion. Don't forsake me. Follow
me.
Follow me, companion, on this wave of anguish.

But my words become stained with your love.
You occupy everything, you occupy everything.

I am making them into an endless necklace
for you white hands, smooth as grapes.

VI. I Remember You As You Were

I remember you as you were in the last autumn.
You were the grey beret and the still heart.
In your eyes the flames of twilight fought on.
And the leaves fell in the water of your soul.

Clasping my arms like a climbing plant
the leaves garnered your voice, that was slow and at peace.
Bonfire of awe in which my thirst was burning.
Sweet blue hyacinth twisted over my soul.

I feel your eyes travelling, and the autumn is far off:
grey beret, voice of a bird, heart like a house
toward which my deep longings migrated
and my kisses fell, happy as embers.

Sky from a ship. Field from the hills:
Your memory is made of light, of smoke, of a still pond!
Beyond your eyes, farther on, the evenings were blazing.
Dry autumn leaves revolved in your soul.

VII. Leaning Into The Afternoons

Leaning into the afternoons I cast my sad nets
towards your oceanic eyes.

There in the highest blaze my solitude lengthens
and flames
its arms turning like a drowning man's.

I send out red signals across your absent eyes
that move like the sea near a lighthouse.

You keep only darkness, my distant female,
from you regard sometimes the coast of dread
emerges.

Leaning into the afternoons I fling my sad nets
to that sea that beats on your marine eyes.

The birds of night peck at the first stars
that flash like my soul when I love you.

The night gallops on its shadowy mare
shedding blues tassels over the land.

VIII. White Bee

White bee, you buzz in my soul, drunk with honey,
and your flight winds in slow spirals of smoke.

I am the one without hope, the word without echoes,
he who lost everything and he who had everything.

Last hawser, in you creaks my last longing.
In my barren land you are the final rose.

Ah you who are silent!

Let you deep eyes close, There the night flutters.
Ah your body, a frightened statue, naked.

You have deep eyes in which the night flails.
Cool arms of flowers and a lap of rose.

Your breasts seem like white snails.
A butterfly of shadow has come to rest on your belly.

Ah you who are silent!

Here is the solitude from which you are absent.
It is raining. The sea wind is hunting stray gulls.

The water walks barefoot in the wet streets.
From that tree the leaves complain as though they were sick.

White bee, even when you are gone you buzz in my soul.
You live again in time, slender and silent.

Ah you who are silent!

IX. Drunk With Pines

Drunk with pines and long kisses,
like summer I steer the fast sail of the roses,
bent towards the death of the thin day,
stuck into my solid marine madness.

Pale and lashed to my ravenous water,
I cruise in the sour smell of the naked climate,
still dressed in grey and bitter sounds
and a sad crest of abandoned spray.

Hardened by passions, I go mounted on my one wave,
lunar, solar, burning and cold, all at once,
becalmed in the throat of the fortunate isles
that are white and sweet as cool hips.

In the moist night my garment of kisses trembles
charged to insanity with electric currents,
heroically divided into dreams
and intoxicating roses practicing on me.

Upstream, in the midst of the outer waves,
your parallel body yields to my arms
like a fish infinitely fastened to my soul,
quick and slow, in the energy under the sky.

X. We Have Lost Even

We have lost even this twilight.
No one saw us this evening hand in hand
while the blue night dropped on the world.

I have seen from my window
the fiesta of sunset in the distant mountain tops.

Sometimes a piece of the sun
burned like a coin between my hands.

I remembered you with my soul clenched
in the sadness of mine that you know.

Where were you then?
Who else was there?
Saying what?
Why will the whole of love come on me suddenly
when I am sad and feel you are far away?

The book fell that is always turned to at twilight
and my cape rolled like a hurt dog at my feet.

Always, always you recede through the evenings
towards where the twilight goes erasing statues.

XI. Almost Out Of The Sky

Almost out of the sky, half of the moon
anchors between two mountains.
Turning, wandering night, the digger of eyes.
Let's see how many stars are smashed in the pool.

It makes a cross of mourning between my eyes,
and runs away.
Forge of blue metals, nights of stilled combats,
my heart revolves like a crazy wheel.
Girl who have come from so far, been brought
from so far,
sometimes your glance flashes out under the sky.
Rumbling, storm, cyclone of fury,
you cross above my heart without stopping.
Wind from the tombs carries off, wrecks, scatters
your sleepy root.

The big trees on the other side of her, uprooted.
But you, cloudless girl, question of smoke, corn
tassel.
You were what the wind was making with
illuminated leaves.
Behind the nocturnal mountains, white lily of
conflagration,
ah, I can say nothing! You were made of
everything.

Longing that sliced my breast into pieces,
it is time to take another road, on which she does not smile.

Storm that buried the bells, muddy swirl of torments,
why touch her now, why make her sad.

Oh to follow the road that leads away from everything,
without anguish, death, winter waiting along it
with their eyes open through the dew.

XII. Your Breast Is Enough

Your breast is enough for my heart,
and my wings for you freedom.
What was sleeping above your soul will rise
out of my mouth to heaven.

In you is the illusion of each day.
You arrive like dew to the cupped flowers.
You undermine the horizon with your absence.
Eternally in flight like the wave.

I have said that you sang in the wind
like pines and like masts.
Like them you are tall and taciturn,
and you are sad, all at once, like a voyage.

You gather things to you like an old road.
You are peopled with echoes and nostalgic voices.
I awoke and at times birds fled and migrated
that had been sleeping in your soul.

XIII. I Have Gone Making

I have gone marking the atlas of your body
with crosses of fire.
My mouth went across: a spider, trying to hide.
In you, behind you, timid, driven by thirst.

Stories to tell you on the shore of evening,
sad and gentle doll, so that you should not be sad.
A swan, a tree, something far away and happy.
The season of grapes, the ripe and fruitful season.

I who lived in a harbour from which I loved you.
The solitude crossed with dream and with silence.
Penned up between the sea and sadness.
Soundless, delirious, between two motionless
gondoliers.

Between the lips and the voice something goes
dying.
Something with the wings of a bird, something of
anguish and oblivion.
The way nets cannot hold water.
My toy doll, only a few drops are left trembling.
Even so, something sings, something climbs to my
ravenous mouth.
Oh to be able to celebrate you with all the words
of joy.

Sing, burn, flee, like a belfry at the hands of a madman.
My sad tenderness, what comes over you all at once?
When I have reached the most awesome and the coldest summit
my heart closes like a nocturnal flower.

XIV. Every Day You Play

Every day you play with the light of the universe.
Subtle visitor, you arrive in the flower and the water.
You are more than this white head that I hold tightly
as a cluster of fruit, every day, between my hands.

You are like nobody since I love you.
Let me spread you out among yellow garlands.
Who writes your name in letters of smoke among the stars if the south?
Oh let me remember you as you were before you existed.

Suddenly the wind howls and bangs at my shut window.
The sky is a net crammed with shadowy fish.
Here all the winds let go sooner or later, all of them.
The rain takes off her clothes.

The birds go by, fleeing.
The wind. the wind.
I can only contend against the power of men.
The storm whirls dark leaves
and turns loose all the boats that were moored
last night to the sky.

You are here. Oh you do not run away.
You will answer me to the last cry.
Cling to me as though you were frightened.
Even so, at one time a strange shadow ran through your eyes.

Now, now too, little one, you bring me honey suckle,
and even your breasts smell of it.
While the sad wind goes slaughtering butterflies
I love you, and my happiness bites the plum of your mouth.

How you must have suffered getting accustomed to me,
my savage, solitary soul, my name that sends them all running.
So many times we have seen the morning star burn, kissing our eyes,
and over our heads the grey light unwind in turning fans.

My words rained over you, stroking you.
A long time I have loved the sunned mother-of-pearl of your body.
I go so far as to think that you own the universe
I will bring you happy flowers from the mountains, bluebells,
dark hazels, and rustic baskets of kisses.
I want
to do with you what spring does with the cherry trees.

XV. I Like For You To Be Still

I like for you to be still: it is as though you were absent,
and you hear me from far away and my voice does not touch you.
It seems as though your eyes had flow away
and it seems that a kiss had sealed your mouth.

As all things are filled with my soul
you emerge from the things, filled with my soul.
You are like my soul, a butterfly of dream,
and you are like the word Melancholy.

I like for you to be still, and you seem far away.
It sounds as though you were lamenting, a butterfly cooing like a dove.
And you hear me from far away, and my voice does not reach you:
Let me come to be still in your silence.

And let me talk to you with your silence
that is bright as a lamp, simple as a ring.
You are like the night, with its stillness and constellations.
Your silence is that of a star, as remote and candid.

I like for you to be still: it is as though you were absent,
distant and full of sorrow as though you had died.
One word then, one smile, is enough.
And I am happy, happy that it's not true.

XVI. In My Sky At Twilight

In my sky at twilight you are like a cloud
and your form and colour are the way I love them.
You are mine, mine, woman with sweet lips
and in your life my infinite dreams live.

The lamp of my soul dyes your feet,
My sour wine is sweeter on your lips,
oh reaper of my evening song,
how solitary dreams believe you to be mine!

You are mine, mine, I go shouting it to the afternoon's
wind, and the wind hauls on my widowed voice.
Huntress of the depths of my eyes, your plunder
stills your nocturnal regard as though it were water.

You are taken in the net of my music, my love,
and my nets of music are as wide as the sky.
My soul is born on the shore of your eyes of mourning.
In your eyes of mourning the land of dreams begin.

XVII. Thinking, Tangling Shadows

Thinking, tangling shadows in the deep solitude.
You are far away too, oh farther than anyone.
Thinking, freeing birds, dissolving images,
burying lamps.

Belfry of fogs, how far away, up there!
Stifling laments, milling shadowy hopes,
taciturn miller,
night falls on you face downward, far from the
city.

You presence is foreign, as strange to me as a
thing.
I think, I explore great tracts of my life before
you.
My life before anyone, my harsh life.
The shout facing the sea, among the rocks,
running free, mad, in the sea-spray.
The sad rage, the shout, the solitude of the sea.
Headlong, violent, stretched towards the sky.

You, woman, what were you there, what ray, what
vane
of that immense fan? You were as far as you are
now.
Fire in the forest! Burn in blue crosses.
Burn, burn, flame up, sparkle in trees of light.

It collapses, crackling. Fire. Fire.
And my soul dances, seared with curls of fire.
Who calls? What silence peopled with echoes?
Hour of nostalgia, hour of happiness, hour of solitude,
hour that is mine from among them all!

Hunting horn through which the wind passes singing.
Such a passion of weeping tied to my bedy.
Shaking of all the roots,
attack of all the waves!
My soul wandered, happy, sad, unending.

Thinking, burying lamps in the deep solitude.

Who are you, who are you?

XVIII. Here I Love You

Here I love you.
In the dark pines the wind disentangles itself.
The moon glows like phosphorus on the vagrant waters.
Days, all one kind, go chasing each other.

The snow unfurls in dancing figures.
A silver gull slips down from the west.
Sometimes a sail. High, high stars.

Oh the black cross of a ship.
Alone.
Sometimes I get up early and even my soul is wet.
Far away the sea sounds and resounds.
This is a port.
Here I love you.

Here I love you and the horizon hides you in vain.
I love you still among these cold things.
Sometimes my kisses go on those heavy vessels
that cross the sea toward no arrival.
I see myself forgotten like those old anchors.
The piers sadden when the afternoon moors there.
My life grows tired, hungry to no purpose.
I love what I do not have. You are so far.
My loathing wrestles with the slow twilights.
But night comes and starts to sing to me.

The moon turns its clockwork dream.
The biggest stars look at me with your eyes.
And as I love you, the pines in the wind
want to sing you name with their leaves of wire.

XIX. Girl Lithe and Tawny

Girl lithe and tawny, the sun that forms
the fruits, that plumps the grains, that curls
seaweeds
filled your body with joy, and you luminous eyes
and your mouth that has the smile of water.

A black yearning sun is braided into the strands
of your black mane, when you stretch your arms.
You play with the sun as with a little brook
and it leaves two dark pools in your eyes.

Girl lithe and tawny, nothing draws me towards
you.
Everything bears me farther away, as though you
were noon.
You are the frenzied youth of the bee,
the drunkenness of the wave, the power of the
wheat-ear.

My sombre heart searches for you, nevertheless,
and I love your joyful body, your slender and
flowing voice.
Dark butterfly, sweet and definitive
like the wheat-field and the sun, the poppy and
the water.

XX. Tonight I Can Write

Tonight I can write the saddest lines.

Write, for example, 'The night is starry
and the stars are blue and shiver in the distance.'

The night wind revolves in the sky and sings.

Tonight I can write the saddest lines.
I loved her, and sometimes she loved me too.

Through nights like this one I held her in my arms.
I kissed her again and again under the endless sky.

She loved me, sometimes I loved her too.
How could one not love her great still eyes.

Tonight I can write the saddest lines.
To think that I do not have her. To feel that I have lost her.

To hear the immense night, still more immense without her.
And the verse falls to the soul like dew to the pasture.

What does it matter that my love could not keep her.
The night is starry and she is not with me.

This is all. In the distance someone is singing. In the distance.
My soul is not satisfied that it has lost her.

My sight tries to find her as though to bring her closer
My heart looks for her, and she is not with me.

The same night whitening the same trees.
We, of that time, are no longer the same.

I no longer love her, that's certain, but how I loved her.
My voice tried to find the wind to touch her hearing.

Another's. She will be another's. As she was before my kisses.
Her voice, her bright body. Her infinite eyes.

I no longer love her, that's certain, but maybe I love her.
Love is so short, forgetting is so long.

Because through nights like this one I held her in my arms
my soul is not satisfied that it has lost her.

Though this be the last pain that she makes me suffer
and these the last verses that I write for her.

The Song Of Despair

The memory of you emerges from the night around me.
The river mingles its stubborn lament with the sea.

Deserted like the warves at dawn.
It is the hour of departure, oh deserted one!

Cold flower heads are raining over my heart.
Oh pit oh debris, fierce cave of the shipwrecked.

In you the wars and the flights accumulated.
From you the wings of the song bird rose.

You swallowed everything, like distance.
Like the sea, like times. In you everything sank!

It was the happy hour of assault and the kiss.
The hour of the spell that blazed like a lighthouse.

Pilot's dread, fury of a blind diver,
turbulent drunkenness of love, in you everything sank!

In the childhood of mist my soul, winged and wounded.
Lost discoverer, in you everything sank!

You girdled sorrow, you clung to desire,
sadness stunned you, in you everything sank!

I made the wall of shadow draw back,
beyond decide and act, I walked on.

Oh flesh, my own flesh, woman whom I loved and lost,
I summon you in the moist hour, I raise my song to you.

Like a jar you housed the infinite tenderness.
and the infinite oblivion shattered you like a jar.

There was the black solitude of the islands,
and there, woman of love, your arms took me in.

There were thirst and hunger, and you were the fruit.
There were grief and the ruins, and you were the miracle.

Ah woman, I do not know how you could contain me
in the earth of your soul, in the cross of your arms!

How terrible and brief was my desire of you!
How difficult and drunken, how tensed and avid.

Cemetery of kisses, there is still fire in your tombs,
still the fruited boughs burn, pecked at by birds.

Oh the bitten mouth, oh the kissed limbs,
oh the hungering teeth, oh the entwined bodies.

Oh the mad coupling of hope and force
in which we merged and despaired.

And the tenderness, light as water and as flour.
And the word scarcely begun on the lips.

This was my destiny and in it was the voyage of my longing,
and in it my longing fell, in you everything sank!

Oh pit of debris, everything fell into you,
what sorrow did you not express, in what sorrow are you not drowned!

From billow to billow you still called and sang.
Standing like a sailor in the prow of a vessel.

You still flowered in songs, you still broke in currents.
Oh pit of debris, open and bitter well.

Pale and blind diver, luckless slinger,
lost discoverer, in you everything sank!

It is the hour of departure, the hard cold hour
which the night fastens to all the timetables.

The rustling belt of the sea girdles the shore.
Cold stars heave up, black birds migrate.

Deserted like the warves at dawn.
Only the tremulous shadow twists in my hands.

Oh farther than everything. Oh farther than everything.
It is the hour of departure. Oh abandoned one!

LIST OF TITLES WITH ISBN NO.

ISBN	TITLE
9788194914129	1984
9789390575220	1984 & Animal Farm (2In1)
9789390575572	1984 & Animal Farm (2In1): The International Best-Selling Classics
9789390575848	35 Sonnets
9789390575329	A Clergyman's Daughter
9789390575923	A Study In Scarlet
9789390896097	A Tale Of Two Cities
9789390896837	Abide in Christ
9789390896202	Abraham Lincoln
9789390896912	Absolute Surrender
9789390896608	African American Classic Collection
9789390575305	Aldous Huxley: The Collected Works
9789390896141	An Autobiography of M. K. Gandhi
9789390575886	Animal Farm
9789390575619	Animal Farm & The Great Gatsby (2In1)
9789390575626	Animal Farm & We
9789390896158	Anna Karenina
9789390575534	Antic Hay
9789390896165	Antony & Cleopatra
9789390896172	As I Lay Dying
9789390896226	As You like it
9789390575671	At Your Command
9789390575350	Awakened Imagination
9789390575114	Be What You Wish
9789390896233	Believe In yourself
9789390896998	Best of Charles Darwin: The Origin of Species & Autobiography
9789390896684	Best Of Horror : Dracula And Frankenstein
9789390575503	Best Of Mark Twain (The Adventures of Tom Sawyer AND The Adventures of Huckleberry Finn)
9789390896769	Black History Collection
9789390575756	Brave New World, Animal Farm & 1984 (3in1)

9789390896240	Brother Karamzov
9789390575053	Bulleh Shah Poetry
9789390575725	Burmese Days
9789390896257	Bushido
9789390896066	Can't Hurt Me
9788194914112	Chanakya Neeti: With The Complete Sutras
9789390896042	Crime and Punishment
9789390575527	Crome Yellow
9789390575046	Down and Out in Paris and London
9789390896844	Dracula
9789390575442	Emersons Essays: The Complete First & Second Series (Self-Reliance & Other Essays)
9789390575749	Emma
9789390575817	Essential Tozer Collection - The Pursuit of God & The Purpose of Man
9789390896578	Fascism What It Is and How to Fight It
9789390575688	Feeling is the Secret
9789390575190	Five Lessons
9789390575954	Frankenstein
9789390575237	Franz Kafka: Collected Works
9789390575282	Franz Kafka: Short Stories
9789390575060	George Orwell Collected Works
9789390575077	George Orwell Essays
9789390575213	George Orwell Poems
9788194914150	Greatest Poetry Ever Written Vol 1
9788194914143	Greatest Poetry Ever Written Vol 1
9789390896301	Gulliver's Travel
9789390575961	Gunaho Ka Devta
9789390575893	H. P. Lovecraft Selected Stories Vol 1
9789390575978	H. P. Lovecraft Selected Stories Vol 2
9789390896059	Hamlet
9789390575022	His Last Bow: Some Reminiscences of Sherlock Holmes
9789390896134	History of Western Philosophy
9789390575121	Homage To Catalonia

9789390896219	How to develop self-confidence and Improve public Speaking
9789390896295	How to enjoy your life and your Job
9789390575633	How to own your own mind
9789390896318	How to read Human Nature
9789390896325	How to sell your way through the life
9789390896370	How to use the laws of mind
9789390896387	How to use the power of prayer
9789390896028	How to win friends & Influence People
9788194824176	How To Win Friends and Influence People
9789390896103	Humility The Beauty of Holiness
9789390896653	Imperialism the Highest Stage of Capitalism
9789390575084	In Our Time
9789390575169	In Our Time & Three Stories and Ten poems
9789390575145	James Allen: The Collected Works
9789390896189	Jesus Himself
9789390575480	Jo's Boys
9789390896394	Julius Caesar
9789390575404	Keep the Aspidistra Flying
9789390896400	Kidnapped
9789390896424	King Lear
9789390575824	Lady Susan
9789390896455	Law of Success
9789390896264	Lincoln The Unknown
9789390575565	Little Men
9789390575640	Little Women
9788194914174	Lost Horizon
9789390896462	Macbeth
9789390896929	Man Eaters of Kumaon
9789390896523	Man The Dwelling Place of God
9789390896349	Man The Dwelling Place of God
9789390575909	Mansfield Park
9788194914136	Manto Ki 25 Sarvshreshth Kahaniya
9789390896509	Marxism, Anarchism, Communism
9789390575664	Mathematical Principles of Natural Philosophy

9788194914198	Meditations
9789390575800	Mein Kampf
9789390575794	Memory How To Develop, Train, And Use It
9789390896486	Mind Power
9789390896585	Money
9789390575039	Mortal Coils
9789390575770	My Life and Work
9789390896035	Narrative of the Life of Frederick Douglass
9789390575152	Neville Goddard: The Collected Works
9789390575985	Northanger Abbey
9789390896530	Notes From Underground
9789390896547	Oliver Twist
9789390575459	On War
9789390575541	One, None and a Hundred Thousand
9789390896554	Othelo
9789390575435	Out Of This World
9789390575015	Persuasion
9789390575510	Prayer The Art Of Believing
9789390575091	Pride and Prejudice
9789390896561	Psychic Perception
9789390575381	Rabindranath Tagore - 5 Best Short Stories Vol 2
9789390575367	Rabindranath Tagore - Short Stories (Masters Collections Including The Childs Return)
9789390575374	Rabindranath Tagore 5 Best Short Stories Vol 1 (Including The Childs Return
9789390896622	Romeo & Juliet
9789390896127	Sanatana Dharma
9789390575596	Seedtime & Harvest
9789390896639	Selected Stories of Guy De Maupassant
9789390575206	Self-Reliance & Other Essays
9789390575176	Sense and Sensibility
9789390575299	Shyamchi Aai
9789390896738	Socialism Utopian and Scientific
9789390896646	Success Through a Positive Mental Attitude
9789390575428	The Adventures of Huckleberry Finn

9789390575183	The Adventures of Sherlock Holmes
9789390575343	The Adventures of Tom Sawyer
9789390896691	The Alchemy Of Happiness
9789390575862	The Art Of Public Speaking
9789390896288	The Autobiography Of Charles Darwin
9788194914181	The Best of Franz Kafka: The Metamorphosis & The Trial
9789390575008	The Call Of Cthulhu and Other Weird Tales
9789390575107	The Case-Book of Sherlock Holmes
9789390896110	The Castle Of Otranto
9789390896745	The Communist Manifesto
9789390575589	The Complete Fiction of H. P. Lovecraft
9789390575497	The Complete Works of Florence Scovel Shinn
9789390896820	The Conquest of Breard
9789390896813	The Diary of a Young Girl
9789390896332	The Diary of a Young Girl The Definitive Edition of the Worlds Most Famous Diary
9789390575701	The Great Gatsby, Animal Farm & 1984 (3In1)
9789390575312	The Greatest Works Of George Orwell (5 Books) Including 1984 & Non-Fiction
9789390575992	The Hound of Baskervilles
9789390896707	The Idiot
9789390896714	The Invisible Man
9789390575657	The Knowledge of the holy
9789390575558	The Law & the Promise
9789390896721	The Law Of Attraction
9789390896776	The Leader in you
9789390896363	The Life of Christ
9789390896196	The Man-Eating Leopard of Rudraprayag
9789390896783	The Master Key to Riches
9789390575268	The Memoirs Of Sherlock Holmes
9789390896479	The Midsummer Night's Dream
9789390575466	The Mill On The Floss
9789390896790	The Miracles of your mind
9789390896660	The Mutual Aid A Factor in Evolution
9789390896448	The Origin of Species

9789390896905	The Peter Kropotkin Anthology The Conquest of Bread & Mutual Aid A Factor of Evolution
9789390896806	The Picture of Dorian Gray
9789390896271	The Picture of Dorian Gray
9789390575275	The Power Of Awareness
9789390896356	The Power of Concentration
9788194824169	The Power of Positive Thinking
9789390575411	The Power of the Spoken Word
9788194914105	The Power Of Your Subconscious Mind
9789390896899	The Power of Your Subconscious Mind
9789390896417	The Principles of Communism
9789390575787	The Psychology Of Mans Possible Evolution
9789390896615	The Psychology of Salesmanship
9789390575732	The Pursuit of God
9789390575398	The Pursuit of Happiness
9789390896851	The Quick and Easy Way to effective Speaking
9789390575947	The Return Of Sherlock Holmes
9789390575138	The Road To Wigan Pier
9789390896981	The Root of the Righteous
9789390575855	The Science Of Being Well
9788194914167	The Science Of Getting Rich, The Science Of Being Great & The Science Of Being Well (3In1)
9789390896011	The Screwtape Letters
9789390896073	The Screwtape Letters
9789390575336	The Secret Door to Success
9789390575695	The Secret Of Imagining
9789390896868	The Secret Of Success
9789390896431	The Seven Last Words
9789390575930	The Sign of the Four
9789390896004	The Sonnets
9789390896516	The Souls of Black Folk
9789390896875	The Sound and The Fury
9789390575244	The State and Revolution
9789390896882	The Story of My Life
9789390896936	The Story Of Oriental Philosophy

9789390896752	The Strange Case of Dr. Jekyll and Mr. Hyde
9789390896943	The Tempest
9789390575916	The Valley Of Fear
9789390575879	The Wind in the willows
9789390896080	The Wind in the willows
9789390575763	Their eyes were watching gofd
9789390575831	Three Stories
9789390896950	Twelfth Night
9789390896592	Twelve Years a Slave
9789390896677	Up from Slavery
9789390896974	Value Price and Profit
9789390896967	Wake Up and Live
9789390896493	With Christ in the School of Prayer
9789390575602	Your Faith is Your Fortune
9789390575473	Your Infinite Power To Be Rich
9789390575251	Your Word is Your Wand
9789390575718	Youth
9789391316099	A Christmas Carol
9789391316105	A Doll's House
9789391316501	A Passage to India
9789391316709	A Portrait of the Artist as a Young Man
9789391316112	A Tale of Two Cities
9789391316747	A Tear and a Smile
9789391316167	Agnes Gray
9789391316174	Alice's Adventures in Wonderland
9789391316136	Anandamath
9789391316181	Anne Of Green Gables
9789391316754	Anthem
9789391316198	Around The World in 80 Days
9789391316013	As A Man Thinketh
9789391316242	Autobiography of a Yogi
9789391316266	Beyond Good and Evil
9789391316761	Bleak House
9789391316778	Chitra, a Play in One Act
9789391316310	David Copperfield

9789391316075	Demian
9789391316785	Dubliners
9789391316051	Favourite Tales from the Arabian Nights
9789391316235	Gitanjali
9789391316068	Gravity
9789391316150	Great Speeches of Abraham Lincoln
9789391316662	Guerilla Warfare
9789391316839	Kim
9789391316822	Mother
9789391316211	My Childhood
9789391316846	Nationalism
9789391316327	Oliver Twist
9789391316853	Pygmalion
9789391316334	Relativity: The Special and the General Theory
9789391316389	Scientific Healing Affirmation
9789391316341	Sons and Lovers
9789391316587	Tales from India
9789391316372	Tess of The D'Urbervilles
9789391316396	The Awakening and Selected Stories
9789391316402	The Bhagvad Gita
9789391316303	The Book of Enoch
9789391316228	The Canterville Ghost
9789391316907	The Dynamic Laws of Prosperity
9789391316006	The Great Gatsby
9789391316860	The Hungry Stones and Other Stories
9789391316433	The Idiot
9789391316440	The Importance of Being Earnest
9789391316297	The Light of Asia
9789391316914	The Madman His Parables and Poems
9789391316457	The Odyssey
9789391316921	The Picture of Dorian Gray
9789391316464	The Prince
9789391316938	The Prophet
9789391316945	The Republic
9789391316518	The Scarlet Letter

9789391316143	The Seven Laws of Teaching
9789391316525	The Story of My Experiments with Truth
9789391316532	The Tales of the Mother Goose
9789391316549	The Thirty Nine Steps
9789391316594	The Time Machine
9789391316600	The Turn of the Screw
9789391316983	The Upanishads
9789391316617	The Yellow Wallpaper
9789391316426	The Yoga Sutras of Patanjali
9789391316990	Ulysses
9789391316624	Utopia
9789391316679	Vanity Fair
9789391316020	What Is To Be Done
9789391316686	Within A Budding Grove
9789391316693	Women in Love